RESURRECTION MAN

Eoin McNamee

PICADOR USA ✖ NEW YORK

Also by Eoin McNamee
The Last of Deeds & Love in History

Picador® is a U.S. registered trademark and is used by St. Martin's
Press under license from Pan Books Limited.

Library of Congress Cataloging-in-Publication Data

McNamee, Eoin
       Resurrection man / Eoin McNamee.
           p.   cm.
       ISBN 0-312-14716-3
       1. City and town life—Northern Ireland—Belfast—Fiction.
    2. Criminals—Northern Ireland—Belfast—Fiction. 3. Belfast
(Northern Ireland)—Fiction.   I. Title.
PR6063.C63R47   1995   95-21825
                                                        CIP

First published in Great Britain by Picador

First Picador USA Paperback Edition: November 1996
10   9   8   7   6   5   4   3   2   1

Critical Acclaim for *Resurrection Man* by Eoin McNamee

"Like great film noir, McNamee's dead-on dialogue and elaborate landscapes of memory and violence will stay with you long after the lights go up."
—L. C. Smith, *Spin* magazine

"An artfully executed tale...a lyrical account of a man in 'pain because of life.'"
—Olivia Tracey, *The New York Times Book Review*

"Fierce and haunting...Intensity and drive...propel the writing."
—Paul Skenazy, *San Francisco Examiner & Chronicle*

"McNamee...offers prose that often rises to poetry.... [His] poetic use of geography gracefully establishes the tenseness of everyday life. *Resurrection Man* is a highly compelling read—a beautiful book about ugliness."
—*San Francisco Review of Books*

"Glorious...McNamee cruises troubled Belfast on the back of a dark angel.... What the reader takes away from this scarifying beauty of a novel isn't so much its body count as its baleful poetry."
—John Domini, *The Sunday Oregonian*

"With bite and brilliance, rising Irish star McNamee burrows deep.... Eerie, memorable...a chilling first-rate debut..."
—*Kirkus Reviews* (starred review)

"Intense mastery of rhythm and image...remarkable for its poetic evocations of violence...This book is a chilling masterpiece and a brilliant debut."
—*Publishers Weekly* (boxed review)

"This is something special.... An extraordinary book."
—Victoria Glendinning

"His prose...is exquisite and surprising, often reaching the pitch of poetry.... A complex, intelligent and morally ambitious novel...McNamee is a powerful and gifted writer, and his first novel deserves to be read—at least as much for the beauty as for the horror."

—Richard O'Brien, *The Times,* Trenton, New Jersey

"It is understandable that a young Irish writer should try to interpret the most traumatic events of his generation. It is remarkable that Eoin McNamee should do so with the poetic instinct and dramatic flair of an old hand."

—Anna Mundow, *Fanfare*

"One of the heavy hitters of the contemporary literary renaissance...the novel is hugely and alarmingly evocative and undoubtedly marks McNamee as a writer of significance.... A dark vision of evil loosed into an already chaotic world...an undoubtedly important novel."

—Colin Lacey, *Irish Voice*

"Takes you into the back streets, the dark places of the soul as well as the city. A combination of mystery and history, the tale of a time and place where dark things happen in the corner, where a man's faith can turn him inside out, where you are always conscious that justice may not win in the end, or what justice is."

—Marilis Hornidge, *The Courier-Gazette,* Rockland, Maine

"A stark, gritty, completely believable book...With this excellent effort, Eoin McNamee has begun his career as a novelist quite auspiciously indeed."

—Mike Hudson, *Irish Echo*

"Achingly exquisite prose as concentrated as poetry, as unfailing an ear for cadences and quirks of Belfast dialogue as Roddy Doyle has for Dublin, and a fatalistic sense of suspense."

—*Sunday Times Magazine*

part one

one

Afterwards Dorcas would admit without shame that having moved house so often was a disturbance to Victor's childhood. But a suspicion would arise in each place that they were Catholics masquerading as Protestants. Her husband James was no help in this regard. He was so backward and shy he needed to stand up twice before he cast a shadow. Dorcas would maintain that Victor did not learn bigotry at her knee even though she herself had little tolerance of the Roman persuasion. She believed that all he really wanted to be was a mature and responsible member of society, loyal to the crown and devoted to his mother. But he suffered from incomprehension. He was in pain because of life.

Dorcas and James came from Sailortown in the dock area. Sailortown disappeared gradually after the war. There is a dual carriageway running through the area now. There isn't even a place where you can stand to watch the traffic. You'd have to get up on a warehouse roof where you might find a lone sniper at dawn, feeling rigorous in the cold and thinking about migration as he watches the traffic, a movement along chosen routes.

The city itself has withdrawn into its placenames. Palestine Street. Balaklava Street. The names of captured ports, lost battles, forgotten outposts held against inner darkness. There is a sense of collapsed trade and accumulate decline.

In its names alone the city holds commerce with itself, a furtive levying of tariffs in the shadow.

James was a dock labourer. He had this deadpan look, a listener to distant jokes. It was like he saw himself as some hardluck figure for whom silence was a condition of survival. Bearing the name of Kelly meant that he was always suspected of being a Catholic. He protected himself by effacement. He was a quiet accomplice to the years of his fatherhood and left no detectable trace.

Sometimes if Dorcas insisted he would take his own son to Linfield matches at Windsor Park. He would get excited and shout at the team. Come on the blues. Victor would look at him then but he would have put the shout away like it was something he'd sneaked on to the terraces under his coat and was afraid to use again.

Once he took Victor up to the projection room during the matinee at the Apollo cinema on the Shankill Road. The projectionist was Chalky White who had been to school with James. Chalky was six feet tall, stooped, with carbon residue from the lamps in his hair and his moustache. There were two big Peerless projectors with asbestos chimneys leading into the ceiling. There were aluminium film canisters on the floor and long Bakelite fuseboxes on the wall. The air smelt of phosphorous, chemical fire.

Chalky showed Victor a long white scar on his arm where he had accidentally touched the hot casing.

'Laid it open to the bone,' Chalky said. He showed Victor the slit in the wall where the projectionist could watch the picture. He talked about film stars he admired. Marion Nixon, Olive Brook. Victor liked Edward G. Robinson and James Cagney in *Public Enemy*. When he looked through the slit he could see Laurence Tierney as John Dillinger laid out on a morgue slab like a specimen of extinction. Flash bulbs went off. A woman said I thought he'd be better looking. Dillinger kept his eyes open, looking beyond the women and the reporters towards his Dakota birthplace, small farms glistening under a siege moon.

James had a photograph of his own father which he kept in his wallet. He was standing with other men in his shift at the docks. They were leaning on their shovels, smoking and stroking their long moustaches like some grim interim government of the dead.

Sometimes when he was watching TV Victor would think he saw his father in the crowd that collected around a scene of disaster. Or standing slightly apart at some great event. Or on the terraces watching great Linfield teams of the fifties and sixties pulling deep crosses back from the byline, scoring penalties in the rain.

After the Apollo Victor worked hard at getting the gangster walk right. It was a combination of lethal movements and unexpected half-looks. An awareness of G-men. During the day he would mitch school and go down to the docks. He would avoid the whores at the dock gate. Their blondie hair they got from a bottle, Dorcas said, and the hair waved in his dreams like a field of terrifying wheat.

Victor spent most of these days behind the wheel of an old Ford Zephyr on blocks at the edge of the dock. The engine had been removed and there was oily grass growing through the wheel arches. It had dangerous-looking fins on the back and chrome bumpers which Victor polished. From the front seat he could see the tarred roofs of goods wagons in the stockyard sidings. Dorcas' brother worked there in a cattle exporter's office. He would sit at their fire at night and talk about cattle, which Victor hated. He had a passion for his work: the bills of lading, statistics of weight loss during transit, mortality rates.

One night when he thought Victor wasn't listening he told Dorcas about finding a Catholic girl in the shed used for storing salt. It was during the thirties. Winter. The wagons were frozen to the rails. The air itself had forceps. The girl and the baby had died in the salt shed with the steam of her labour above her head and the cord uncut between her thighs. When they found her they sliced the cord with the blade of a shovel. When they lifted her they saw salt crystals stuck to her thighs like some geodic shift quarried for her in the moment of her death.

Victor sat at the wheel of the car until dusk most nights. He preferred it when it began to get dark. By day the city seemed ancient and ambiguous. Its power was dissipated by exposure to daylight. It looked derelict and colonial. There was a sense of curfew, produce rotting in the market-place. At night it described itself by its lights, defining streets like a code of destinations. Victor would sit with the big wheel of the Zephyr pressed against his chest and think about John Dillinger's face seen through a windscreen at night, looking pinched by rain and the deceit of women.

It was dusk when Trevor Garrity and Alan McAtee from school found Victor in the car. Garrity sprang the bootlid and looked inside. McAtee went to the driver's window and looked in. Victor had a sense of frontiers, a passport opened to the raw, betrayed face of your younger self.

'How's Pat?' McAtee said. He was three years older and had bad teeth which Victor couldn't stand.

'My name's Victor. Pat's a Taig name.' He wondered how Edward G. Robinson would handle this. Later he would realize that men had been doing this for centuries, stopping each other in remote places, demanding the credentials of race and nationality.

'Kelly sounds like a Taig name to me,' McAtee said casually. 'Your ma must of rid a Taig.'

'Come here till you see this,' Garrity said. McAtee went to the back of the car. Victor followed him. He kept most of his private possessions in the boot and Garrity had emptied them all out onto the ground. There was a scout knife with a fake wooden handle. Twenty Gallagher's blues with a box of matches from the Rotterdam bar. A Smirnoff bottle opener. A copy of *Intimate Secrets Incorporating Married Woman* that Victor had found. When he heard Garrity at the boot Victor expected to lose something. The cigarettes. The knife. Instead he saw that Garrity had the magazine.

'Come here till you see this,' Garrity repeated. McAtee stood beside him and began to read over his shoulder.

'Fuck me, my hubby couldn't believe . . .'

'His wicked love potion drove me . . .'

'I felt a shudder through my most private zone . . .'

'My secret Taig lover by Mrs Dorcas Kelly.'

Victor reached for the knife on the ground. McAtee put his foot on it.

'Pat didn't like that.'

'Pat's sensitive about his ma.'

Victor waited. He could see the shapes of violence laid out in his head like a police diagram with skid marks leading away.

He learned that there was a pattern to such moments. A framework of inconsequential detail. When he took the first blow on the side of the head and went down he was thinking about the last moments of gangsters. He had a sudden awareness of texture and temperature. He understood about people talking about the weather at funerals. He imagined being a gangster and seeing a cockroach or a metal fire escape or something else they had in America. Garrity kicked him in the crotch. A shudder most private. The magazine lay open on the ground beside his head. The Wife of the Month had long yellow breasts, half-hidden, which she seemed to offer in consolation. Her mouth was open as if she was about to utter mysteries, messages of explicit loneliness directed at him. Must of rid a Taig.

They moved to so many districts it didn't seem to matter what Dorcas thought. To rear a son in such a selection of streets did not donate stability to his life; however, she did her best. Victor always took up with older boys, men sometimes, who were not concerned about his moral welfare. He was always in trouble, and she possessed no means to stop it. She thought it was a wonder how she managed to survive this life at all. Pregnant at age seventeen and having to marry in such haste she could barely walk up the aisle with dignity. She thought sometimes she might have married a shadow or a ghost, James was so quiet. She did her duty by him, although there were times she felt an awful emptiness of regret. It was necessary to have firm beliefs to get by. She remembered that Victor wrote to her often of his childhood when he was in prison, always starting his letters 'dear mother' and ending 'yr loving son'.

By age twelve Victor was in trouble for larceny and shop-breaking, led down that path by his elders. She talked to the magistrate with spirit and he got the benefit of the Probation Act that time. James his father never came near the court. She accepted nothing from Victor that was not got honest, and he was always there with small gifts, which is why she wondered at the newspapers – sometimes they printed such lies.

Victor later befriended Garrity and McAtee. He showed them how you could take bus passes off younger pupils and sell them on. Victor would stop someone at the school gate. McAtee would hold them and Garrity would beat them. Victor watched the eyes. It was a question of waiting for a certain expression. You directed a victim towards gratitude. You expected him to acknowledge the lesson in power.

People learned to be obsequious, to defer to him. This led to problems of isolation. He believed he knew how Elvis felt.

After school he would walk down to University Street where he would wait for the Methody girls to come out wearing the compulsory black stockings and high-heeled shoes. They took lessons in deportment, sexual gravitas. Their skirts were worn an inch above the knee and stocking seams were checked with a steel ruler for straightness. They took make-up classes resurrection man

where they learned how to obscure vital faults and arouse precise longings. They were deeply aware of their own attractions. They knew how to prolong moments of anticipation. Lace brassières were visible.

Their fathers would gather in University Street to drive them to their homes outside the city. They performed this task unsmilingly. They avoided looking at the legs of their daughters' classmates and greeted each other with stern nods only. They possessed their daughters as if they were branches of obscure knowledge. There were things that were penetrable only to fathers of beautiful girls, exclusive sorrows.

Afterwards he would go down to the Cornmarket to listen to the preachers and their recital of sectarian histories. They were thin men dressed in black with ravaged faces. They predicted famine and spoke in tongues. Their eyes seemed displaced in time. They would eat sparsely, sleep on boards, dream in monochrome. There was a network of small congregations and merciless theologies throughout the city. Congregations of the wrathful. Baptist. Free Presbyterian, Lutheran, Wesleyan, Church of Latter-day Saints, Seventh Day Adventists, Quakerism, Covenanters, Salvationists, Buchmanites. Pentecostalists. Tin gospel halls on the edges of the shipyard were booked by visiting preachers for months in advance. Bible texts were carefully painted on gable walls.

Victor listened to their talk of Catholics. The whore of Rome. There were barbarous rites, martyrs racked in pain. The Pope's cells were plastered with the gore of delicate Protestant women. Catholics were plotters, heretics, casual betrayers.

When he went home he would find his father washing in the kitchen and Dorcas watching television. *This Is Your Life*. Dorcas would ask where he had been.

'Down at the Cornmarket.'

'Them preachers. In America they have them preachers on the television.' His father walked in, drying his neck.

'You'd better mind yourself, Victor. End up saved, so you will,' he said.

9

Victor and Dorcas turned to look at each other. James stared over their heads at the television, his inattention cancelling the spoken word.

'Did you hear something?' Dorcas asked Victor.

'Never heard a thing, ma.'

James opened the back door and went out. He kept pigeons at the back. Dorcas said he spent more time with the pigeons than he did with his own family. He never even spent time watching television with them, but moved from one region of silence to another.

'Your da has me tortured,' she said.

'Never mind, ma,' Victor said. 'That guy ain't going to do nothing to you, dollface.' Dorcas laughed.

'Me and yous going to fill that guy full of lead, blow this town.'

Dorcas loved it when Victor talked like this big gangster from the films, but there were times when she would discipline him with a stick in the yard. She remembered that she would be beating Victor and James would cross the yard as if they were not there. Sometimes she thought that what her husband had was a kind of madness. Later Victor read books on it in the Crumlin Road prison, and told her about the different forms of mental absence.

She worried about Victor when she read the letters about madness. They included words that she could not pronounce. Long words whose meaning could only be measured with the aid of finely calibrated and lethally expensive instruments. She could not imagine the consequences of such words. Psycho-pathology. She wondered if such words were dangerous to Victor.

In 1969 the streets began to come alive for Victor. They appeared in the mouths of newsreaders, obscure and menacing, like the capitals of extinct civilizations. Delphi Avenue. He got a delivery job driving a lorry. During the day he would memorize a street, the derelict sites, no right turns, areas strangely compassionate under street-lights. He'd listen to the BBC in the cab. Unity Flats, Kashmir Road. The names took on an air of broken glass, bullet holes circled by chalk, burnt timber doused by rain. He felt the city become a diagram of violence centred about him. Victor got a grip on the names.

On his day off Victor would go down to Crumlin Road magistrates' court. Park the car and then go in, women looking at him. It was a gift he had. Detectives would nod at him in the foyer. Looking good, Victor. It was the quiet respect of the interrogation room, the promise of darker days ahead. Victor sat in the public gallery beside the relatives as the defendants were called in. He liked to see a Taig brought into the box, a man's thin figure wearing a cheap leather jacket and a V-neck jumper. He hated the Taig women sitting beside him. Their anxious looks which he despised. Their air of somebody sitting on a cardboard suitcase on a deserted railway platform, in flight from one half-starved city to another.

He drank in the details of a crime, in particular the ornate details of route and destination. He studied the type of weapon used, barrel rifling and trajectory. The pathologist's report with photographs of entry and exit wounds was handed round the court and he followed its intimate passage from hand to hand.

Lastly there was the testimony of witnesses: I just seen these blue flashes in his hand and the deceased just kind of sat down, I can't explain it. The testimony of detectives from Delta or Charlie division. The kind of look they put on for the judge made Victor laugh. Like, I'm haunted by dates of civil unrest, your honour.

Victor could have any woman he wanted. Click his fingers. But the women only lasted one or two nights. They'd look into his face when they were alone with him and get frightened. Looking into Victor's blue eyes when you were fucking was like watching a televised account of your own death, a disconsolate epic.

He reckoned that Heather was the only woman who ever understood the depth of his ambition. He would always go back to her during the good years. Besides, Victor liked a woman with meat, pockets of flesh you could put your hand into. Towards the end she'd drink Bacardi and cry like hell itself. But at the start it was all Jesus, Victor, I could eat you with salt. Her big slow voice. Come on, you big fucker. I'm dying for a fuck. Take you home and fuck you bendy.

Dorcas said that Victor's favourite programme was Harry Worth. He'd split his sides laughing, she thought he'd burst a vessel. He was always crackers about cars also. His first was a Mk II Escort with wide wheels and this hand you stuck in the back window that waved hello. Big Ivan thought that was the cat's pyjamas. Him and Big Ivan would go down to the car park on the Annadale Embankment, do handbrakes in the gravel.

Before he formed his own unit Victor sat in on several killings. In one they picked up a Catholic on the Springfield Road in a hijacked black taxi. He got a bit of a digging in the back and was moaning by the time they got him to a lock-up garage off the Shankill. They carried him inside. There was an acetylene torch in the corner of the garage. A battery leaked acid on to the floor. Victor wore a blue boiler suit and carried a shortblade knife that he'd got in the Army and Navy stores. There was a smell of butane in the air, a sense of limits reached.

The body was found in a shop doorway on Berlin Street. There were 124 careful knife wounds on the body. Death was due to slow strangulation. The victim appeared to have been suspended from a beam while he was being stabbed. The taxi was found abandoned on waste ground. There were traces of blood on the windows and a woman's lipstick under the passenger seat.

two

There was a cellophane-wrapped ordnance map of the city above Ryan's desk in the newspaper office. He spent hours in front of it. Locations of sectarian assassinations were indicated by red circles. Many of these represented call-outs, the phone ringing late at night and a drive across the city through checkpoints. He would reach the place in driving rain. There would be a scene-of-crime officer, fingerprint and forensic men. The forensic men had fine hair and glasses. They wore white boilersuits and rarely spoke. They approached a corpse with gravity, removing it to another context.

There were lines on the map too, indicating rivers, areas which had been demolished, suggested escape routes following a bomb, zones of conflict, boundaries, divisions within the heart. Ryan drew a new one on the map almost every day. An evolution had been going on in there over the past three years, a withdrawing behind the lines. He thought he could learn something by keeping a record of encroachments and retreats. He was trying to develop the knowledge that the inhabitants of the city had. The sense of territory that guided them through hundreds of streets. That feeling for the anxious shift in population. He stared at the lines and circles that proposed something beyond the capacity of maps. His markings were like the structure of a language. He expected to hear its guttural sound being pronounced on the streets. He imagined being addressed in it. It would be arcane, full of sorrow, menacing.

Ryan had been working with Ivor Coppinger for two years. Coppinger was more deeply involved. It was Coppinger for instance who conducted meetings in parked cars with off-duty police and UDR men. There were intricate relationships involved once the contact was made. Knowledge became a form of suffering. In the end the information became almost incidental. Coppinger listened to terrible things about ambition, parenthood.

Early that morning he had gone with Coppinger to the Albert Bridge. A chemical tanker had been parked on the bridge with a bomb on board. He got to the scene just as the area was being sealed off. They were waiting for someone from the fire brigade to identify the cargo. The lorry was on the pavement with its hazard warning lights on. The man from the fire brigade could not read the cargo labels without binoculars. While someone went for them they stared at the orange decals at the back of the tank, symbols of mass panic and death by inhalation. The bomb disposal men were moving slowly up the Albert Bridge Road, pausing at intervals as if they were aware of other signs, not easily detectable: a shift in the breeze, a magnetic tug of warning in the currents of the Lagan beneath the bridge. Before they reached the lorry the detonator had gone off without piercing the tank. The man from the fire brigade said afterwards that it contained dry-cleaning fluid.

Coppinger had told him about Constable McMinn and Frames McCrea. McCrea had crashed through 164 checkpoints in stolen cars. McMinn had been picked to catch him because he was a part-time rally driver. There was a network on the outskirts of the city to which he belonged. Sullen men working in garages, stripping engines on oil-soaked benches, grinding down valves, increasing ratios, moving towards devout moments of speed and power. Small local papers carried intense motor-sports coverage, photographs of morose champions.

McCrea had become a matter of legend. He was at the centre of mystical events. The cars he stole had been peppered with bullets. He had jumped a checkpoint ramp and landed on the Stockman's Lane motorway access. He stopped outside Tennant Street RUC station every night and held the horn down to provoke a chase.

When McMinn rammed him off the road in Amelia Street the reaction was extreme. Two nights ago McMinn and his partner were dragged into the Victoria bar. They were forced to crawl on their hands and knees. They had to walk like chickens. McMinn was taken into the toilets where a shot was fired into the wall beside his head. He was forced to eat shit.

Coppinger pointed this out as an indication of the feelings aroused. The deeply felt immunities of the hero had been breached.

That afternoon Coppinger put the medical report of the first knife killing on Ryan's desk. After death the head had been almost severed from the trunk. There were two depressed fractures of the skull, fragments of glass embedded in the face. The root of the tongue had been severed.

Later that afternoon Ryan drove Coppinger out to the scene.

'They would've parked the car there,' Coppinger said, pointing to the mouth of a small alley.

'Drag marks,' Ryan said, examining the pavement. There were bloodstains against the wall. There was nothing to distinguish the bloodstains or the doorway where the body had been left, but they both had a sense of familiarity, of scenes repeated in history.

'They would have done your man out of view in the alley,' Coppinger said, his finger describing their progress, 'dead or near enough.'

'He was strangled, cut to pieces.'

'I reckon they kept him alive though, until they got here. They wanted him to know who was doing it.'

Ryan followed Coppinger's thinking. The point of a random sectarian killing was its randomness, but here the killer wanted to be known to the victim. He wanted to convey familiarity. The cry of the victim as a form of address. The killer would demand ritual. He would sever the throat regardless of arterial blood. He would hold the knife aloft.

Ryan found himself thinking about the way Margaret used to mutter in her sleep at night. She would mention unironed shirts, a room which needed wallpaper. Interior conversations composed of oceanic trivia which left him feeling sleepless and adrift.

'The head was attached to the body by tissue at the back,' Coppinger said. 'It near fell off when he was moved.'

There was a certain awe in his tone. There was someone out there operating in a new context. They were being lifted into unknown areas, deep pathologies. Was the cortex severed? They both felt a silence beginning to spread from this one. They would have to rethink procedures. The root of the tongue had been severed. New languages would have to be invented.

three

Heather waited for Darkie Larche in the top room of the Gibraltar bar. There was sunlight coming in through the dusty windows and she put her legs on a pile of pamphlets to catch it. She loved the sun like life itself. Any chance she got she'd smear herself in oil and sit out in the Ormeau Park like some Buddha you saw in a book. She felt a voracious tenderness in the sun. She dreamed of beaches in Spain, high-rise hotels, oiled bodies that gave you the daytime sadness you felt for those who died young. Children with wasting diseases, teen-age girls in car crashes.

The television was on in the corner with the volume turned down. She wasn't like the other women who came into the bar, watching every news they could in case their street would appear. They looked on TV like a navigation system, migrating home through the channels. She watched scenes of street violence with the volume turned down. It gave her a sense of survival that she liked. Darkie called it the body count and watched it to check on incidents that his unit had been involved in. He would shake his head in sorrow at inaccurate details; a victim's age given wrongly. It implied a lack of respect, an improper observance of the formalities. It was somehow vital to him that a victim's age, religion and the exact location of the hit be given precisely. Errors were subversive. They denied sectarian and geographic certainties.

The room was filled with metal filing cabinets and unopened piles of literature. It was Heather's job to ensure that these were distributed. Glossy pamphlets with full-colour pathologist's photographs of bomb victims were sent anonymously to politicians and journalists. The reds and blues of exposed veins and mutilated fatty tissue reminded her of Twelfth bunting. Packing them in envelopes she felt like the organizer of a sad parade.

Other pamphlets were more conventional. For God and Ulster. No Surrender.

Darkie came in, looked at the television and went to the window. He had brown skin and high cheekbones, remnants of a Huguenot merchant ancestry. He was continually nervous with a kind of racial edginess, the dissenter's fear of pogrom. He came over to the desk and flicked at the pile of pamphlets with the tip of a ruler. He moved behind Heather and slipped a hand into the opening of her blouse, fingering her breast as if he had come across a mislaid object. Heather had often come across this kind of sexual absentmindedness in members of various organizations. And she remembered it in two young British intelligence officers she had met at a party the week before. Soft-eyed boys with north-country accents who disappeared together into a back bedroom as soon as they arrived, then stood around shyly afterwards, their trembling lips a little open as if they were on the verge of making secret disclosures, revelations of fellatio.

'Take your blouse off,' Darkie said, keeping his eyes on the television. She felt him shift his grip and remained still. 'This fucking Victor Kelly character has that lot downstairs in fucking palpitations. Take your blouse off.'

'Make me. Who's Victor Kelly?'

'This character hangs round the Pot Luck with Big Ivan Crommie and Willie Lambe. Thinks he's God's gift to the movement. Word is his da's a Catholic. Thinks he's some kind of hard man. Shooting the mouth off about how the only way to do someone is with a knife, for fuck's sake. Take it off or I'll rip it.'

'Take her easy, Darkie, it's only new. So what's the citizens' army so worried about?'

'Don't be so fucking sarcastic. They're all scared out of their shite of him for some reason. My fucking granny's ninety, has palpitations if she wins ten bob at the bingo. This lot's supposed to be a unit. Defenders of the faith and all. Are you going asleep on me or what?'

'What's your big mad rush anyhow?'

'Supposed to be a council meeting at six. Look very professional, so it would, them walking in and me sticking it in for God and for Ulster. Look at them bastard politicians on the TV – us down here doing their dirty work for them.'

'If you're going to do it, do it right. It's not a fire you're poking.'

'Say it was him that cut this poor fucking Taig to pieces with this knife. Boy they found on Berlin Street.'

'Who did – put your hand there.'

'Victor Kelly, I told you. My granny . . .'

'What?'

'I says my granny . . .'

'Fuck your granny.'

She liked Darkie. He was sensitive to the pain his organization inflicted. He watched funerals on the news, commented on the age of the children following the cortège. He had a sense of obligation. He was committed to a wider vocabulary of death which included widows and children. She liked his inattention, his slim brown cock, his seriousness.

She left him in the office and went downstairs where she ordered a Bacardi at the bar. There was still sunlight coming through the windows and the sandbagged doorway. Late afternoon. The sound of traffic. City centre office workers dispersing to their homes on the outskirts with the radio turned up high for news of diversions, checkpoints in the radial suburbs.

The barman had to say her name several times before she took her change. It was a quality in her that women disliked. A lack of focus. A physical memory dwelt on.

There were four or five men in the corner of the bar talking about guns.

'I could get you this Lee-Enfield. Perfect nick. Come across in the *Claudia*.' The *Claudia*. The turn of the century arms smuggler, a potent name riding in the offshore currents of an empire's memory. Source of arms, blockade runner, succourer of outposts.

'Lee-Enfield my arse. Tell us this, how do you hide a rifle in a fucking crowd? The pistol's your only man. The revolver. Smith and Wesson.'

'Browning.'

'Fucking Magnum.'

One of the men detached himself from the group, joined his hands and arched his back. The others stopped talking and watched. He straddled an imaginary victim lying on the ground.

'This way you see into his eyes.'

He lowered his joined hands until they were within a foot of the ground and moved as if from recoil.

'Keep looking in the eyes. Boom. Fucking brains out.' The man lifted the front of his shirt and mimed pushing a weapon into his waistband, then stepped back to the bar and lifted his drink.

'That's fucking all right close up. What happens you want to plug the bastard from the roof. Out a window?'

'That takes your SLR, your Armalite, your Kalashnikov.'

'Not the fucking Lee-Enfield's been sitting in your ma's attic this past fifty years getting blocked up with mouseshit.'

They were appreciative of the mechanisms of death. Some of them were ex-soldiers and had travelled to places such as Cyprus, Belize. Their sentences had a dusty, travelled air, a patina of hillside ambushes and jungle airlifts that the others respected. They wore highly polished shoes and saluted with pride at the cenotaph on Remembrance Sunday. On Saturday morning at dawn they took groups of men outside the city for small-arms training.

They cultivated the carefully selected victim, economy of movement, the well-aimed single shot to the head. They were in control of their hatred. It was a tactical asset. They were worried about the young men coming into the organization and their dependence on random structures.

Over the following year most of them were interned on the HMS *Maidstone* moored in the lough, or in the prefabs of Long Kesh. They accepted this, lived by army discipline and spent their days constructing a rueful politics, things that prisoners work at alone in their cells, improvising in solitude.

Heather had slept with one of them when she first came to the city. He had taught her some Malaysian words in the bar. The word for where. The word for how much. She spoke them to him in the back seat of his car. She imagined him in a foreign brothel pointing to her. I'll take that one. Leading her upstairs. The laughter from other rooms. The malarial silences.

She had been brought up in a seaside town twenty miles from the city. There was a network of these towns stretching along the coast from the city. During the summer people from the city stayed in guest-houses and littered the dunes with bottles and sandwich wrappers. Their arrival each bank holiday was momentous, a movement of populations. A desperate trek with ten-mile tailbacks. Sacrifices were being made, hardships endured.

In winter the town was empty, sand blowing in the car parks. She went drinking in the dunes with hollow-eyed local boys. The front was deserted. She liked walking there, inventing reasons why there was no one in the town any more. She imagined herself the sole survivor of an epidemic, a vast contamination of loneliness. Clouds massed along the skyline. Tidal surges left large boulders on the breakwater and drift-wood in the outdoor swimming pool on the promenade. Walking on the front she could feel the sea grinding against the concrete beneath her feet. She tried to decipher voices in the sea. She thought she could detect a vocabulary of forces. At home she listened to the shipping bulletins, lying in bed at night with a transistor beside her, stations inching their way off the air with mariners' jargon.

She moved to the city at eighteen and worked in bars. She began to move towards the loyalist pubs. The Pot Luck, Maxies, the Gilbraltar. Men smiled at her. Hey, big tits. She took a flat above a Chinese restaurant and beside a hairdresser's on the Lisburn road. The smell of perming lotion leaked through the floorboards and walls. In the evening Chinese men played cards in the yard of the take-away surrounded by chickens in plastic freezer bags. They talked softly to each other in Chinese, a rivertongue of strange gamblers she felt familiar with. She would lean on the window-sill listening to them, voices in a dim light, a vernacular darkness which seemed lit by the yellow chickens defrosting in trays.

Ryan rang the police press office to confirm the details of the Berlin Street killing. They said they had no details. Cause of death to be established. A language of denial was being employed. His editor refused to accept the story without confirmation.

'I saw him in the morgue,' Ryan said. 'He was cut to ribbons.'

'Get confirmation.'

'They won't confirm. They'll wait a year on the inquest finding. His head nearly fell off when they lifted him.'

'Come back to me on it tomorrow.'

'Story's dead tomorrow. It was like he had these long cuts all over his body. Hundreds of them. You could tell he was alive when they cut the throat. A witness says he heard someone saying kill me, please just kill me.'

'OK, write it up.'

The story did not appear in the morning edition. It was not the first time this had happened. Ryan thought he detected a failure of nerve, a reluctance to admit the terrible news.

After work he went to the Europa hotel. It was one of the first places to introduce body searches at the entrance. The hotel was bombed regularly. It had most-bombed-hotel status. Ryan had noticed increased local awareness of the value of such detail. Most-shot-at police station. Contempt was expressed for quiet areas.

Ryan went into the Horseshoe bar and ordered a drink. He watched the foreign correspondents come in. Photographers in khaki shirts with big pockets. Older men in safari jackets who looked continually dazed. It was said they had trouble distinguishing between assignments. One of them had told him that other wars kept creeping into his reports. His memory was swamped with incident. The presidential palace is surrounded. Armed gangs are roaming the commercial sector. There were long silences when he read these reports down the phone to his night editor in London. At a nearby table another group of English journalists was drinking heavily.

'I saw the bomb in Woolworth's today.'

'It's his first bomb.'

'You stand around for hours and then it goes off. The building just collapses silently and then the sound hits you. There's something comic about it.'

'It's a sonic delay. The blast travels faster than the sound. The blast is over by the time the sound gets to you.'

'The fucking building collapses and there's no noise. Then boom. It's like it was staged. Like Buster Keaton was going to walk out of the dust or something.'

'Did you ever smell gelignite. It smells exactly like marzipan. Cake mixture.'

'There was a lot of dust. I never thought of dust. Flames yes.'

'Women in aprons. Orange peel. Glacé cherries.'

*

Coppinger came in and ordered a pint of Bass. He'd been drinking in Tiger Bay. Listening to stories about the Blitz, Kingdom Brunel in Belfast, the construction of the *Titanic* in the shipyard. He said that a cousin of his father's had accidently been sealed in the *Titanic*'s double hull and the body had never been found. It was a haunted ship, he said. There was a ghostly tapping below the waterline.

Ryan followed his gaze towards a small group of men in a corner of the bar. Two of them he recognized as paramilitaries. The other two were unfamiliar but they had a military air about them. They could have been arms dealers. Ex-army steeped in counter-terrorist lore. The effect of rapid fire in an urban warfare situation. Arranging consignments of weapons from Rotterdam warehouses in crates marked machine parts. Kalashnikov. But Coppinger pointed out that the clothes were wrong.

'A quartermaster's notion of what you wear drinking in a hotel bar. Sports jackets, two, tweed. Ties, matching.'

Meetings like this were taking place all over the city. Fields of operations were defined. Documents of safe passage were granted. Information was exchanged. At official level these meetings did not take place. Accusations of army collusion with paramilitary groups were vehemently denied but the army continued to negotiate at ground level. People were aware of levels of duplicity being created. Irrational guilt complexes were being reported by doctors. The level of heart disease and road death was under investigation. Coppinger said he had difficulty in maintaining an erection. Teenage suicide was on the rise.

Ryan's thoughts turned back to the knife murderer. He considered the idea of an evangelist with burning eyes, a seeker after fundamental truths. Stripping away layers with a knife to arrive at valid words. Please. Kill me.

'Place is coming down with pros,' Coppinger said, indicating a fair-haired girl standing at the bar. She saw him and moved towards them. There were freckles between her breasts and her nipples were visible beneath her blouse.

'Your headlights is on,' Coppinger said when she came up beside them.

Ryan thought for a moment about taking her home. He had an urge for feigned desire. He wanted to hear an invented language of sex, its expressions of forgetfulness and terror.

When they left it was raining. The city centre was always empty after five o'clock. Street lighting was sparse as if areas of darkness had been agreed. You got a feeling of single cars cruising the streets with sinister gleams from their windscreens. Drizzle falling from a vigilante sky.

four

Sometimes Victor would take Big Ivan and Willie Lambe on a night-time tour. It was a game he liked to play. He would sit in the back of the car with his eyes closed and tell them where they were. They argued about how he did it. Big Ivan said it was the sense of smell. Bread from the Ormeau bakery, hot solder near the shipyard, the hundred yards stink from the gasworks. Big Ivan reckoned that he mapped the city with smells, moving along them like a surveyor along sightlines. Willie thought of pigeons homing. Migrations moving to some enchanted and magnetic imperative.

Driving in and around the Shankill his recitations became more ambitious. He knew the inhabitants of every house and would tell their histories, give details of women's lives lived on the intricate margins of promiscuity. This was the bit that Willie liked. Victor always had a ride on his arm. He told them about the forty-five-year-old schoolteacher who waited for him dressed as a widow. Or Sawn-off, the sixteen-year-old with inverted nipples. Big Ivan was haunted by this idea. He tried to imagine the nipped ends. It was part of the imagery of women which scared him. Part of hosiery, bra sizes, the language of B-cup, D-cup, something he couldn't cope with. He thought about women's ironic conversations in changing rooms. Terrifying dialogues carried out over the lingerie counter in Anderson and Macauley's department store. Fifteen denier. Sheer.

Sometimes when they stopped the car outside the Pot Luck or Maxies Victor would stay in the back seat, his lips

ith hot pokers was found in a quarry on the Black
had discovered in them the transcendent possi-
ent suffering. They did not know how to express
a member of the Aryan brotherhood and had a
zi memorabilia at home. Swastika armbands, SS
officers' chevrons. He knew the importance of
they were invested with secret energies and
of transformation. He understood the Nazis'
anguage into power.
ather was against the parties. Darkie explained
ey were necessary. Various strands had to be
er, introductions arranged, informal contacts
e. She could understand that. It was the fact
vas involved that worried her. She suspected
another agenda. He was in there from the start,
problem, some kind of deep thematic disturb-
n't put her finger on.
v,' she said. 'It's like McClure, it's like you woke
d dream and you can't remember what it was
scared the shit out of you and then you see
remember.'
t that Darkie would laugh when she said that
this kind of shy grin which worried her.
before the first party Darkie arrived at nine
ansit van. Heather was in bed and had to get

ck, Darkie,' she said, 'it's only nine o'clock
g, girl needs her sleep.'
d his hand quickly into the gap of her dressing
to the van and came back carrying a case of
key. She had a sudden feeling about the rest
t a man who came to her house every week
breast as if it was necessary to register a
t her heart, a password. She looked out and
r piled on the pavement.
a fucking army or what, Darkie? Is there a

moving. It was an inventory of the city, a naming of parts. Baden-Powell Street, Centurion Street. Lonely places along the river. Buildings scheduled for demolition. Car parks. Quiet residential areas ideal for assassination. Isolated gospel halls. Textures of brick, rain, memory.

Joining the UVF put him in touch with Big Ivan, Willie and others. Onionhead Graham. Hacksaw McGrath. He learned about serious money. First of all just going into shops and taking things. He learned that he didn't have to threaten. Shopkeepers were glad to hand over goods. He was relieving them of hidden fears, split-second images of wives and children being confronted by masked men. Then he started going on to building sites and offering protection. He believed they would sleep better by paying him. No-warning bombs were frequent. People were being gunned down in the street. He was offering them a place in random events and always made a point of calling at the same time every week. He was the means by which they could align themselves to unpredictable violence.

With his first real money he bought a black Ford Capri from Robinson's showrooms. Robinson gave him the nod when it came in. Here's a 007 for Victor he said, a fucking Bondmobile. He hinted at lethal extras, hidden blades, machine-guns behind the headlights. He was a gifted salesman and knew what Victor wanted. He regarded car showrooms as centres of subliminal knowledge. People lowered their voices instinctively. The lighting was austere and respectful. The cars were tended daily by mechanics in white overalls. He would open the car door and invite the customer to enter the interior with its smell of imitation leather, polish and warm plastic. He wanted them to feel dazed and exalted. He picked out the Capri for Victor because it had suggestions of power and generosity. It implied little margin for error, lives on the edge.

Victor was in Maxies the night they got John McGinn. They

had picked him up earlier on the Crumlin Road. Maxies was to be the Romper Room. The name was taken from a children's television programme where the presenter looked through a magic mirror and saw children sitting at home. You sent in your name and address if you wanted to be seen through the mirror. The magic mirror had no glass. It was thought to contain secrets of longevity. It gave you access to the afterlife.

'What's your name?'

'John.'

'John fucking who?'

'John McGinn.'

'Through the magic mirror today we can see John McGinn. Hello John. We'll call you Johnnie. Do your friends call you Johnnie? We're your friends.'

We share your sense of bewilderment. Your intense loneliness. You were in a hurry walking down the Crumlin Road. You were going to work, to a night class, to meet a woman in a bar. We can hear her crying because you didn't turn up. We share her sadness. We will be a comfort to her.

'Over to you Victor.'

'Fucking butterfingers.'

'Hey, he near broke my foot. He's got something hard in there.'

'It's his fucking skull.'

'He levitated. I swear to God he levitated over the bar. He's a magician or something.'

'Here's a message for the fucking Pope.'

Billy McClure was the first to use the Romper Room. He was familiar with forms of initiation. He had convictions for paedophilia and knew that complicity was everything. It was a question of maintaining a ceremonial pace with pauses and intervals for reflection. There had to be a big group of participants. Twenty or thirty was good, particularly if they were close-knit. That way you could involve whole communities. You implicated wives and children, unborn generations. The reluctant were pressed forward and congratulated afterwards.

'Good man, Billy.'

'I seen teeth coming out them on the floor over there.'

'You can come around ou digs any time, Billy.'

There were long pauses the bar eager to buy rounds was ignored. He lay on the and the pool table. There scalp. Victor would wander McGinn with his boot and s specimen of extinction.

Later Victor would se structure. The men settled They took their jackets off whole range of sounds cou third stage came around breathing was laboured. disappointments. Futility

At 4 a.m. Victor took his throat.

Heather found out late suggested the parties in Every time he saw her he look made her think of their bodies abraded by made her think of unb tives. He would arrive at silent boys. Skinheads. and Wrangler parallels visible beneath the stu or smoke. Their serious

Darkie told her l mentally handicapped

old marked Mountain. H bilities of si pain. He wa roomful of N cap badges, insignia, ho possibilities extension of

At first He to her that t brought toge had to be ma that McClure that there wa an underlying ance she coul

'I don't knc up after this b except that it McClure and yc

She thoug but he just gav

The mornir o'clock with a up to let him in

'What the Saturday mornr

Darkie slipp gown then went Black Bush whis of her life. Abo and touched he palm print agair saw crates of be

'We expectir

new regiment in town or what? Maybe it's all for me? Maybe this is a message I'm drinking too much or something? Would you mind telling us what you're at?'

Darkie was in the lounge moving furniture to the sides of the room.

'Darkie, this is getting on my tits so it is.'

He was absorbed in engineering the party. Wide open spaces in the middle of the floor, intimate niches near the windows, easy access to the bedroom. He put a framed photograph of her father into a drawer and moved a standard lamp from one corner of the room to another then pulled the curtains to see the effect. Heather felt the room flooded with innuendo.

She was upstairs getting dressed when she heard the doorbell. She looked out of the window and saw a telephone engineers' van parked at the kerb. She heard Darkie opening the door. Minutes later he came in through the bedroom without knocking. There were two men wearing overalls behind him, one of them carrying a box with a khaki telephone attached. They inspected the room as if she wasn't there. One of them then said 'behind the bed' in an English accent.

'Darkie.'

'They're here for the phone is all. Come on with me, get some breakfast. I'm fucking starving so I am.'

The parties were held every Saturday night. Most of the time Heather did not know the people who arrived or how they knew her address. She studied her front door for cryptic marks like in a book. In the end she became accustomed to opening the door to well-spoken Englishmen in suits, off-duty policemen, senior figures in the UDA and faces she recognized from the television. Sometimes there would be men she recognized from the Gibraltar coming in awkwardly like barbarian chiefs from the outlands bringing with them a smell of cooking fires and fresh blood.

The policemen would gather in the kitchen where they talked about guns: rates of fire, target density. Nervous conversations conducted in an edgy dialect of ballistics. They got drunker than anyone else and held quick-draw competitions with side-arms in the hallway.

The Englishmen in suits would wait for the arrival of McClure with the boys. He took the boys into a bedroom and made them wait. A staged delay hinting at complicated preparation. The men fixed each other's ties and began to make small feminine gestures. The group seemed to be strengthened by their shared anticipation so that when McClure came out and waved the first one into the room a murmur of gentle encouragement came from the others. Heather thought they looked like candidates for interview. That McClure and his boys were waiting behind the door to probe them on the significant regrets of their lives, to debrief them of crucial sorrows.

They emerged with their heads down, walking gently as if escorted from the room by some disconsolate presence.

Darkie would go drinking in local discos to bring back new girls. They were always impressed by the cars parked outside the flat. RS2000s, Opel Mantas in rally spec, Escorts with wide wheel arches and magnesium alloy wheels. Things to conjure with. Rich paintwork suggesting the visionary landscape of the showroom catalogue. The UDA men were popular with these women. They carried wads of cash in their hip pockets and played money games with the girls, inserting twenty-pound notes into apertures in their clothing. It was all obvious. Nothing was left to chance. The girls' squeals and gestures of denial were artificial. There were overtones of family violence, red-eyed fathers beating their daughters wlth belts. Occasionally one of them would move away from a man and smooth her skirt down primly. The man would gaze sullenly into space. A sign that he had left out a detail of the flirtation.

On the third Saturday night a girl did a striptease on the living-room floor. A retired sergeant from the B-Specials used a torch as a spotlight and men tried to pull her on to their knees. Once she had taken her blouse off there was a seriousness to her movements as though she was trying to piece together a precise sequence of arousal from remembered fragments. A boy who held her against the wall and whispered. The smell of rain. She turned away from her audience, her hips moving, unfastening the strap of her white bra. Heather wanted to touch her narrow back, its discovered grace. She thought about words you used when you were young. Promise you won't tell if I let you. I never let nobody before.

Often towards morning Heather would come across one of the Englishmen leaving the bedroom, shivering, and with his eyes blank as though he had just returned from a journey in which he carried the unbearable news of his own death.

Drinking in the Botanic Inn Ryan had a phone call telling him to meet Coppinger in the Gasworks bar on the Ormeau Road. Walking through the University area he detoured through Chlorine Gardens to Stranmillis where he had lived with Margaret. There had been several visiting professors and a television producer living in the same street. There was a small coffee shop where their wives gathered in the morning and Ryan had gone there sometimes to listen to them. Conversations he imagined you would hear at embassy parties in the eastern bloc or foreign compounds in Gulf states. The inadequate grasp of local politics, talk of staff becoming sullen and unco-operative, the belief in the army's ability to maintain order on the streets. There were symptoms of bewilderment and a fear of last-minute evacuation.

The windows of the Gasworks bar were covered with wire mesh. You entered through an unlit corridor of sandbags. Heads turned towards the door when he entered the bar. Ryan felt suspect. There was no sign of Coppinger. As soon as he walked in he knew he was going to be singled out. He had trouble summoning the correct responses. It was a question of assembling an identity out of names: the name of school attended, the name of the street where you lived, your own name. These were the finely tuned instruments of survival. He lurched towards the toilets. Inside he leaned his head against the wall in front of him while he pissed. The sound of running water was deafening, ruinous. He read the word Adamant stamped on the massive Victorian urinal. The name had a monumental quality. It had the strength of great certainties. Cast-iron, porcelain. The men who installed it built bridges, gasworks, canals. They were capable of assessing the qualities of a material, its interior conviction, and measuring it against their own. Brass taps, lead pipes. He heard a voice behind him, almost inaudible over the sound of flushing water. He waited to be pushed against the wall and interrogated, realizing it was a mistake to leave the crowded bar for this place which dealt in functional truths, and it was a minute before he recognized Coppinger's voice.

'Fuck's sake, I reckoned you'd be skulking in here scared out of your shite, Ryan, you big girl's blouse you.'

They sat in a corner away from the bar. Coppinger pointed to a sheet of fake wood stuck roughly over the bar.

'There's bullet holes behind that,' he said. 'Fuckers opened fire through the window last month.'

Ryan had noticed people pointing out bullet marks and bomb sites. They added to the attraction of the city. Bloodspots on the pavement were marked by wreaths. Part of a dark and thrilling beauty.

Coppinger was talking about the knife killing. He had been given a list of possible names for those involved. His informant had insisted that he did not write them down. They had to be committed to memory. Coppinger had sat for an hour in a parked car on the Ormeau embankment chanting names until it seemed that the recitation was an end in itself, a means of fathoming the forces at work. As if the knowledge they were looking for was concealed in the names themselves. It seemed possible. It was a clear night. There was mist on the river and the words in his mouth became strange. He could have been naming distant galaxies. He began to detect elemental properties in these words devoid of their associations, the dense tribal histories attached to a name.

'Who was mentioned?'

'Darkie Larche. Onionhead Graham. Mostly Darkie's crew. Problem is something like this isn't Darkie's style.'

'Any idea where they're operating out of?'

'The usual places were mentioned. The Pot Luck. The Gibraltar. Maxies maybe.'

'Anything else?'

'Not a whisper. People's jumpy as fuck on this one. You ring the peelers even and you talk to someone who won't give their name and they pass you on to some other bastard won't give his name and they put you on to the press office who says that investigations is continuing.'

'Are they pursuing a line of enquiry? Are they looking for anyone in particular? The driver of a blue car seen in the vicinity? A woman walking her dog near the scene? A woman walking her dog'd be a good witness. It's something to do with kindness to animals and regular habits.'

'Nothing like that. Nobody round here sees nothing no more. Even a woman walking the dog's looking the other way.'

'Give me some of those names again.'

'Darkie Larche. Onionhead Graham.'

'I don't know, where do they think they are? Chicago in the twenties? Maybe we should be looking for information from the fucking FBI, the fucking Pinkertons. Maybe it's just the police know fuck-all, sounds like they know fuck-all.'

'It's like everybody's frightened, the peelers and all. Even the hard men's worried. Word is you mention the subject to them they go buck mad. Like don't remind them. Hard enough to find out things as it is but this one's buried far as everybody's concerned. I don't know why you're so worried. There's enough going on every day to keep you busy for a month, even if you do find something out you've got an editor won't touch the stuff if it was money and I think he's right. Like nobody wants to read about it. Like nobody wants to see pictures of starving darkies on the TV. Somebody gets shot they don't mind so much. It's like the poor shot fucker could've got out of the road if he'd any sense and not stood in front of guns going off. Or maybe it's like he must of done something to deserve it. There's something official about getting shot with a gun. It's like the gas chamber, fucking guillotine. It's kind of legitimate. Like once you got a gun you got to have somebody to shoot at. Load the magazine, pull the trigger and whatever you're having yourself. But people don't want to read about maniacs cutting people up with knives.'

'You're wrong there. I know you're wrong. People love to read things like that. Innocent victim of sex fiend. Lapping it up. Sexual organs mutilated. Policemen with thirty years' experience controlling their emotions.'

'You're right. There's nothing like a set of mutilated sexual organs.'

'Or a partially undressed corpse. Signs of recent intercourse.'

'Like the slut must of done something to deserve it.'

'We're getting away from the point.'

'Are you looking for a conspiracy theory here.'

'Nothing like a good conspiracy theory when you're drinking in a bar, you don't know if you're going to get yourself shot for walking in the door just.'

'A cover-up at the highest level'd be better.'

'Fuck you.'

'Seriously.'

'Seriously fuck you.'

*

Ryan left Coppinger at the bar and emerged cautiously on to the Ormeau Road. To be seen coming out of the Gasworks could formally identify you as a target. You looked for cover. You watched the headlights of oncoming cars, staring into the filament. Engine notes were important. Military vehicles had a high-pitched diesel whine which made you think of curfew breaches, peremptory orders to halt, unexplained gunfire in the night. Even the sound of his own feet seemed illicit. He thought about the file of blurred photographs at the paper of those who disappeared without explanation. Photographs taken at birthday parties, family gatherings. A sense of the inevitable about the self-effacing smile. Something is being masked, the bitter knowledge that they will soon find themselves lost in the untenanted houses of the dead.

five

Dorcas said it was true she did conceal worries about Victor in her heart as anyone would. There was so much going on in the way of shootings and killings being committed on a regular basis and much of it covered up by government order as well. Though James once said not to worry, you had more chance of getting yourself hurt in a road crash or accident at work as you would have of getting shot — and he could prove it by statistics which surprised her. He could surprise you like that, she said, in the way he usually said nothing you thought he didn't know what was going on. She knew for instance he concealed a passionate nature once, though you wouldn't think it to look. It was a case of still waters.

But Victor had this gift to make you laugh. Even when he was young he could have you in stitches by mocking the neighbours or acting the big gangster he saw in the pictures. But there were times you would see an anger and a darkness there so that he would fight often with other children. He had as many sides to his nature you couldn't keep up. But he never raised his hand to her in all his born days nor would any son that loved his mother, though on occasions she put a strap to his backside taking no pleasure from it but being driven by a grim necessity of duty. When he was a child sometimes he would cry for no reason, which she understood as it was a frequent occurrence of her own nature, just starting for no reason when she was at the washing line or salt tears pricking her eyelids suddenly when she was out shopping so that at times she was driven to refuge in a public toilet in the city centre to stay there with the tears tripping her.

He had an eye for the women too. That was his father in him she thought. She had the opinion that women were an undue influence in his life. He was forever watching after them the way they walked and all. She reckoned that woman Heather had a hand in his destruction. To look at her you'd have thought that butter wouldn't melt. He said to Dorcas he could laugh with her which is what attracted him. She said to him she knew what attracted him: the big Zeppelins she had on her and the little girl voice. But she found him heedless of her concern although when he was visiting he left her outside in the car. She could see he was in a fog of lust with her around and said to him once did she come with a warning like a prescription from the chemist: do not drive or operate heavy machinery? It was a case of an old story at work from the start and he knew it not being able to look her in the eye.

After a job Victor would meet with the others in the Pot Luck to watch the evening news. It was an early ambition of his to have a job as first item on the news but then he became distrustful of the narrative devices employed. The newsreaders' neutral haircuts and accents, the careful placing of stresses to indicate condemnation or approval, the measured tones of reassurance. The suggestive, shifting vernacular used left Big Ivan more confused than anyone. He heard accounts of events he had been involved in which conflicted with his experience. He felt that rich portions of his memory were being snatched from him. Victor wondered if this had anything to do with Big Ivan's sudden conviction that he had been adopted at birth. He would read aloud stories of children abandoned in telephone boxes with scrawled notes describing their tiny marginal lives. One night he told Victor that he knew what his real parents were like. His father was tall and handsome. His mother had a resonant and ageless beauty, but both were concealers of a secret grief. Victor put on a face of concern when Big Ivan spoke of this, though in his private thoughts he considered that if he had been the father of a baby in the likeness of Big Ivan he would have abandoned if not strangled it.

When the unit's activities were mentioned on television Willie Lambe would give himself over to an uncritical delight. He imagined himself in later years being interviewed in front of the camera. His confident grasp of the issues raised. His early life. He would admit to dark times, lean periods when he struggled with despair but then explain the benefits of an optimistic nature and share insights gained through hardship. He would praise the role of family life.

That March Victor was asked to carry out a kneecap job on three members of the organization who had burgled an elderly woman's house. It was a question of discipline and maintaining the image of the organization. He knew that the men involved were members of the Gibraltar bar unit. Darkie Larche's men. It would be necessary to arrange a meeting in the Gibraltar to get clearance for the punishment. He didn't like this. He knew how Larche would react. The great Victor Kelly looking for permission. He could see Larche standing at the bar going this Kelly character doesn't know his arse from a hole in his trousers has to come to me and ask permission. Victor would walk into the Gibraltar and Larche would laugh and slap him on the back. Like he was some big friend. Hey, you behind the bar there, give my mate Victor a drink there, your fucking arm broke or something? The great Victor Kelly, come on with that drink there, your fucking leg tied to the piano?

When he had set up the meeting Victor planned the job down to the last detail. It was almost as if the punishments had been carried out. When he shut his eyes it was like watching a film with the volume turned down. He could see men bundled into a car, their faces obscured, brought to a secret location. The interrogation. The blue muzzle flash. He could see himself being driven away from the scene with the face of a man troubled in his heart. He thought that this must be what they called a premonition.

The meeting took place in the top room at the Gibraltar. Darkie Larche was there with three older men from the area. Victor sat down at the table. Darkie said nothing. The three older men looked like the frail members of a government in exile, deeply versed in the politics of failure. Victor put his case simply, projecting an air of humility. He listened while the three men gave the matter grave deliberation, reached agreement in principle. Darkie did not speak.

Downstairs Victor insisted on buying the drinks. A group of younger men gathered around him and he sensed that the three older men were uneasy in his presence. His sports jacket with checks that cost ninety pounds, his ability to cause bursts of nervous laughter, the deadly vacancy in his eyes. Occasionally Darkie looked across the room and raised his glass to him. Later in the night he called for silence in the bar. He said that he was pleased to see Victor there and welcomed the new spirit of co-operation. That Victor was welcome to join the Gibraltar unit at any time. He said that he himself did not personally believe rumours to the effect that Victor's father was a Catholic. The silence in the bar was maintained. Everyone was looking at each other with an awareness of hidden weapons. They knew that the insult could not go unanswered. The young men stepped back from Victor and the group around Darkie rearranged itself imperceptibly. Victor observed the way they all changed position, the choreographed movements leading towards a duel. He felt detached, interested in the outcome. This was an ability he had, to step outside himself, think on different levels. He had a sense of dusty main streets, the clink of spurs. Going to the pictures he had learned respect for the western showdown. Men working from necessities buried deep in their nature. The brief exchange of words as an acknowledgement of men puzzled beyond endurance. The heat. The formal desolation. Two men feeling marooned in the hinterland of their own desire. The smell of leather, gun oil and sweat.

Victor stepped away from the bar wondering how he could get to the Browning under his jacket. He could see the butt of a revolver in Darkie's belt. Then he felt the attention of the room shift to the door behind him. Risking a glance he saw Willie Lambe standing there with a police issue Walther in his hand. Suddenly everyone had guns, people were moving between him and Darkie. He considered taking out the Browning, blazing away. He could feel the three older men around him, talking gently, moving him towards the door.

'Car's waiting, Victor.'

Heather saw Victor for the first time at one of the parties. He came in with two others. The first thing she noticed was his black curly hair and dark skin so at first she thought that he was foreign, a sailor off one of the boats. She had a weakness for men with foreign looks. He looked like he might think in another language. She wondered if he might be an Arab. She had read somewhere that Arabs liked plump women and she imagined him discussing the plumpness of women in a strange and cruelly shaped alphabet. He looked like a man who carried within a tense coil of stored words capable of describing rare and dangerous sexual acts. The congress of the snake.

When Darkie came in she asked him who he was. Darkie barely looked towards him.

'Dangerous territory. That's the famous Victor Kelly. Flash bastard. Thinks he's God's gift to women, sun, moon and stars shine out of his fly.'

'I thought he was a foreigner,' she said, giggling.

'Could say that, supposed to be his da's a Taig from the Falls.'

'They say Taigs is good at it.'

'Don't.'

'What?'

'Just fucking don't.'

'What are you looking at me like that for?'

Darkie had a sensation of faint recollection as if he was twenty years from that moment and stirred by a particular memory.

'What look?'

'That kind of sad parting look. That fond farewell look. Kind of all the good times we had together sort of a look.'

'I haven't a baldy what you're on about.'

Since the parties had started she had seen less of Darkie during the week. When they met he was reluctant to touch her as though the time they had spent together was inscribed on her skin, faint outlines easily erased. He subjected her to long silences so that she had become an authority on the types of male silence. There were silences of sorrowful reproof. Fond silences. Dumb silences. Doubtful silences. Nursing of wounds silences. There were the profound viral silences belonging to the terminally ill.

'Introduce me.'

'What?'

'I have to say everything twice to you these days. Introduce me. I want to meet him.'

Heather knew he would refuse. Later she approached the group by the window. They were talking and laughing among themselves in the alcove formed by the velvet curtains she had bought herself in Corry's. Darkie said she was picking whorehouse furnishings but she didn't care. She loved the touch of the red fabric and the way it made you want to rub against it.

The three men stopped talking and looked up as she came towards them. It was like an oriental scene from a film she had watched. Suddenly she felt as if she could go down on her knees, make ritual gestures of submission and repentance. The other two were impassive, unimpressed by the way she found herself walking, swaying from the hips, eyes downcast. Victor moved sideways on the sofa to make room for her. She sat down.

Later she said he had these blue eyes could see right through you. After a while she noticed that Big Ivan and Willie Lambe were drunk out of the mind. It was like the way they were most of the time, locked, so that they hardly knew what they were doing. Not Victor. He was Mr X-Ray with this good smell off his leather jacket and aftershave, a bottle of which he kept in the glove compartment of his car, a new one every week. His personal habits were very good also. He gave her a cigarette and took one and lit them both with a gold Dunhill lighter. But he was hardly what you would call a smoker, she said; he would spend his time looking along the butt like it was a gun barrel or blowing smoke rings to make you laugh like some-body's uncle, but it was really like a cigarette was something he found dropped from the sky he didn't know what to do with.

She said that it wasn't hard to guess from the way she talked that she was smitten straight off which was the God's honest truth not something she ever wished to hide. She was mad for him like no other man. He could make her cream herself just by looking. She said she could have had him there on the sofa or anything and you could tell he felt that way too. Without a word being spoken they went to the spare bedroom which she kept locked at parties because of a horror of walking in on a couple which would make her feel used in her own body. Before they got in bed he took out this big gun he had stuck in his belt and spun it around in his hand all the time watching himself in the mirror on the wardrobe with an expression of being somewhere else completely, until she said to him come here, please, hurry up. I can't bear it.

*

Afterwards they went for a drive in his car. Victor always had energy, a terror of sitting still. Sometimes Heather saw him act like an escaped prisoner with involuntary backward glances as if there were dogs on his tail. They moved carefully among the sleeping bodies on the living-room floor. Victor made a game of it, pretending to stumble and put his foot in some-one's mouth, bringing it down an inch to the side of the person's head. He did this in slow motion so Heather could hardly bear it, choking back giggles. She had a feeling that McClure was awake and watching them. Nothing she could put her finger on. Just somebody's eyes open, a glimpse of intrigue in the dark.

Dawn had broken. There was a fine drizzle falling and Heather laughed at the way rain beaded in Victor's hair like a hairnet you'd see an old woman wearing. He took a firing position outside the house and pretended to shoot down a seagull. His hand described it falling, arcing across the city. He made the sound of a crippled engine with his lips, the sound of a fuselage crumping on impact, exploding in a blaze of aviation fuel. Games. They drove slowly about the city. At first Heather thought he was driving at random; then she saw the pattern. He was driving carefully along the edges of Catholic west Belfast. She had never been this close before although she had seen these places on television. Ballymur-phy, Andersonstown. The Falls. Names resonant with exclu-sion. Now they were circling the boundaries, close enough to set foot in them. Victor drove up into the foothills until they were looking down on the west of the city, its densely popu-lated and mythic new estates, something you didn't quite believe in. He looked down at it then turned to her. You never ask what where I've been or what I've been doing, he said. Never. You don't even think, he said. Yes, Victor, she said. He stopped the engine and reached for her. She thought he wanted to do it within sight of the enemy. He pointed out different parts of the city to her. New Lodge. The Short Strand.

He described how you could wipe them off the map from here. Artillery fire directed with precision. Repeated sorties. She could feel his excitement at the idea. He saw himself as a general conducting pre-dawn briefings with a roomful of men with drawn faces, targets circled on a map. He pulled her towards him and undid the buttons on her blouse then slipped his hand inside her bra without unfastening it so that he could feel the floral pattern at the top pressing into his hand. They stayed like that, her head turned towards him with a kind of disbelief in her eyes. The nylon left a mark on the back of his hand which did not fade until that afternoon. A ceremonial motif, relic of some half-forgotten rite.

Later that day Willie Lambe and Big Ivan picked up Jimmy Craig, Ian Morris and Frames McCrea for the burglary. They brought them to the back room of the Pot Luck where they waited for Victor. The atmosphere was relaxed. Big Ivan went to the bar to get twenty Embassy Regal for Ivor Morris. The Pot Luck team were courteous, enquiring after wives and girl-friends. They apologized for the drab surroundings and the delay in Victor's arrival. They spoke among themselves in hushed, sympathetic tones. Willie Lambe kept looking ner-vously at his watch and Jimmy Craig reassured him. Take her easy there, Willie. We know Victor's kept busy, man can't be in two places at once. Frames McCrea was the only one who said nothing. After Frames had got out on bail he had started to look old. His forehead was deeply lined. He suffered from waking suddenly at night, intimations of mortality. It seemed as if he had discovered an exhausting and terminal truth while he was in full flight through the city centre in a stolen car. One hundred and sixty-four checkpoints. People pointed him out in the street. The site where he had launched the car over a checkpoint on to the motorway ramp was visited by children, and he had not developed the means to fend off their awe, the grim reticence of the exalted and solitary.

The mood changed when Victor came in. He wanted a flawless exercise he said. He was talking in terms of operational details. He had arranged for three separate cars to be waiting outside and that someone be waiting at the lock-up garage where the kneecappings were to take place. He talked about integral planning. He had adopted an officer's stance, legs apart, his hands behind his back holding the Browning loosely. He talked about the robbery. An innocent old woman robbed in her home then tied up and left alone until a neighbour released her. The joint pains. The thoughts of her grandchildren, their bright and eternal faces under blond hair and her uncertain efforts to retain their names. He talked about the evening sun shining in through her bedroom window on to the faded wallpaper. His voice was kindly and reproachful. Craig and McCrea hung their heads but Ian Morris looked him straight in the face.

'We never done it, Victor,' he said, 'we never done a thing like that.'

Victor nodded to Big Ivan who hit Morris with his fist on the side of the head. Willie Lambe hit Craig. Big Ivan kicked McCrea. Victor continued. The three men had spent the day in the Gibraltar buying drinks from the proceeds of the robbery. The barman had described the notes smelling of mothballs. The money the old woman had kept to pay her funeral expenses, a bitter-scented currency of dissolution. Willie Lambe hit Craig backhanded. Big Ivan kicked Morris in the kidneys and headbutted McCrea.

'Me and you's mates, Victor,' Morris said. 'You know me. I wouldn't go and rob one of our own for fuck's sake.'

'Fucking graverobbers,' Big Ivan said, knocking him over.

'Old lady could of died, fucking circulation suffocated the fuck out of her tied up like that,' Willie Lambe said, thinking about his own mother, the way her feet got cold at night.

Victor knew that it could go on like that all day. He stepped forward and put the barrel of the Browning against each man's forehead in turn and told them they had thirty seconds to tell the truth and shame the devil. The gun barrel left a mark between each man's eyes and their faces were tense and fixed so that they looked like the members of a sect devoted to moments of urgent revelation. In the end it was Frames McCrea who gave them the details. It was a spare account. They had ignored the fact that they would almost definitely be caught. This blindness, he seemed to be saying, had led him to question his motives. Craig entered a plea for clemency. Morris turned to Willie, pointed at his temple with a forefinger and raised his eyebrows. Willie shook his head, smiling.

'No problem Ian. No nut jobs today. We're just drilling kneecaps.'

The three men were escorted outside and into the cars. Big Ivan, Hacksaw McGrath and Victor were to be the firing party. Willie Lambe had to leave to bring his mother to the shops. Big Ivan was annoyed at the inclusion of Hacksaw. Hacksaw was a mad dog, Big Ivan said. Victor explained that Hacksaw needed to be blooded as part of a precision operation.

On the way to the garage Victor talked to Ian Morris about greyhounds. Morris was an acknowledged expert and had formulated a plan for introducing Arab racing dogs to the city's tracks. He kept two of them in his backyard. Salukis. So far they had refused to let him get within five yards of them. He had been brooding on this, watching them from the kitchen window, the fine-boned disdainful way they had of walking, their lack of proper import documentation. He imagined them running at Dunmore Park, describing the anatomy of a desert wind in heart-stopping record circuits. Victor was sympathetic.

Inside the garage there were three clean revolvers sitting neatly on a workbench. A rotating Castrol sign moved gently on its axis when they entered. McCrea seemed relieved to enter the familiar gloom, strewn with car-parts, a place devoted to the principles of dismantling. Victor told them to lie face-down on the floor. Craig said that he didn't want to ruin the new suit he had bought the week before. Big Ivan pointed out that he was going to shoot him through the trousers anyway. This hadn't occurred to Craig. He lay down, grimacing as he lowered his body on to the floor. Victor told the Pot Luck men to stand over each one and wait for his signal. They were to fire a single shot into the back of each knee. He paused for a moment to permit a gathering of thoughts.

Afterwards he would wonder in private what was going through Frames McCrea's head. Whether he had seized on some imaginary reserve of immunity left over after Constable McMinn had knocked him sideways off Amelia Street into the side of a parked lorry where he had stayed with his head resting on the wheel and the speedometer jammed at eighty-three until firemen arrived to cut the clutch pedal from around his foot. Perhaps the circumstances had awakened the impulse to flight that had led him towards stealing cars in the first place. Victor saw him get to his feet and look around slowly. Victor was surprised to see a faintly aggrieved look that he had seen on his own mother's face often. It expressed resentment at the encroachment of life and of the memories she had made for herself, their slow accumulation and drag. He began to run towards the garage door. To Big Ivan it seemed as if he had discovered another gravitational field within the confines of the garage. His legs seemed to be moving with the same buoyant steps that men with bulky suits had made on the moon. Out of the corner of his eye Victor saw Hacksaw raise his revolver and aim with the preoccupied and stately air of a child sighting on an imaginary Indian. He shot McCrea once in the back so that he fell forward on to his face and lay without moving. Victor went over to inspect him then told the others to resume their positions, reflecting that you only ever achieve an approximation of what you desire.

six

Artie Wilson was transferred from Crumlin Road to the Down-shire Hospital with a psychiatric report stating that he was suffering from paranoid delusions. He thought that someone was going to kill him. Staff at the Downshire tried to reassure him. They explained to him that the hospital doors were locked against killers that might stalk his nights. Allegorical figures with shuffling walks and pale speculative eyes. They under-stood his fears. There is something about an institutional corridor which lends itself to raw fear. The shining tiles. The antiseptic distances.

Wilson, who was from the Village, had been convicted of selling cartridges for an unlicensed shotgun to a Catholic and given two years. The two men had shared receding memories of duckhunting at dusk on Lough Neagh. Crouched in a punt offshore waiting for the clipped arctic beat of wings coming towards them out of the darkest part of the October sky, until it seemed a kind of grace to be there as witness to vast and incurious migrations from the North. They knew there had to be consequences. Wilson had asked to be held in solitary confine-ment in Crumlin Road prison to protect him from the loyalist prisoners. It gave him time to think about the nature of betrayal. He borrowed books about the great traitors from the prison library. Lundy, Casement. It seemed to him that his own error in consorting with a Catholic was minor compared to these men whose deceits were concerned with the future of nations.

At the Downshire they counted the knives after dinner and

locked up toxic paints after art therapy class which led him to think about suicide. On television he watched pictures of girls who had been tarred and feathered for going out with British soldiers. They were left dangling from lampposts like crude fetishes designed to ward off a vengeance of intimate proportions. He remembered having seen it happen in the Village to a girl who was engaged to a Catholic. The women had shaved the girl's head indoors while the men stood around outside with the tar and feathers, smoking and chatting. It seemed a form of initiation prescribed by custom.

When he was returned to Crumlin Road he would lie awake at night in the pilgrim darkness waiting for the metal shutter of the judas hole to slide back.

At the beginning of September he was released on two weeks' parole. At home he was quiet and reflective, attentive to his family and to his parole officer. He was surprised at how difficult it was to find his way back to his old life. It seemed to be a thing requiring skills of navigation accompanied by prayers and invocations and he was ignorant of them. On his last night he opened the front door to a smiling man in a black leather jacket who said he wanted to buy a shotgun.

'You must have the wrong house.'

'I don't think so. It's not a bad evening. Good for shooting.'

'I suppose.'

'Ducks.'

'Too much glare. They'd come in at you out of the sun before you knew where you were,' Artie Wilson said, knowing he was lost.

'Or Taigs.' There was a black Capri on the other side of the road with another man leaning on the bonnet looking at him with the kind of passionate disinterest people reserve for victims of serious car accidents lying on roadside verges. Victor took a revolver out of its pocket and pressed it to Wilson's side just below his heart.

'Or traitors,' he suggested in a whisper.

*

In Castlereagh Interrogation Centre Victor was fingerprinted then photographed front and profile. Looking good, Victor. He knew that these photographs were important, that in the future they could be released to the press. When he took a comb out of his pocket and smoothed his hair back none of the policemen objected. There was a silent acceptance of his sense of privilege. He was escorted from room to room gently. He began to suspect that they had a good case against him.

He was brought to an interview room. He recognized the detective who entered.

'How's about you, Herbie. Haven't seen you this good while. Thought you was transferred.'

'I seen you though, Victor. I was keeping a wee eye out for you.'

Victor laughed out loud to show he was aware of the direction things were taking. That he knew how policemen were attracted to the ominous statement.

'You're a hard nut, Victor, isn't that right?'

'See my new motor when you were watching me, Herbie? The Capri?'

'I suppose you're going to tell me where you got the money to buy it?'

'That's right, Herbie, I'm going to break down and confess.'

'I know you are Victor. You're going to cry like a baby and tell us you wish you never done it, you just don't know what come over you.'

'Capri's a flying machine, Herbie. Give us a shout someday, I'll give you a run in her.'

Each man chose his words carefully. They knew that ordinary speech was inadequate to the occasion. The exchange was carefully staged. At the start they were using the tones of flawed irony employed in gangster films, weary and laced with knowledge of the relentless nature of human greed and cruelty. Later they would move towards the process of questioning, a language of lovers prone to nuance and revelation, sensitive to pain.

'You're a good-looking boy, Victor, a real charmer.'

'You know how it is, Herbie.'

'We got some eye-witnesses in a line-up downstairs to admire you, Victor. Women and all. Just dying to get a look at the great Victor Kelly. Seen you do Artie Wilson, so they did. I'm sure you won't object.'

'You know me, Herbie, always willing and eager to help the law.'

'This won't take a second, Victor.'

Victor joined four other men in the identification parade. The others all wore leather jackets, cheaper than the one Victor had. The brightness of the room highlighted the lines on their faces. They exuded an air of disappointment, unfulfilled lives. Somewhere it seemed they had been found wanting and brought, haggard and unshaven, to this windowless room, a place of unwavering judgement. There was a stir when the eye-witnesses were brought in. They waited in the darkness behind the bright lights. Victor could sense their attentiveness, the way they held their breath in the face of the choice they were about to make.

'Face front.'

Victor turned into the lights and gave them a dangerous smile which he had practised in front of the mirror. It was a Cagney smile, elegant and derisive. It showed that he had invulnerability to spare. Then he began to walk towards the lights. At first no one reacted. The other men in the line-up exchanged glances. He stepped in front of the lights and peered into the darkness with one hand shading his eyes. He looked bewildered now, deprived of familiar landmarks. Two uniformed policemen grabbed him from behind.

'I'm fucking innocent,' he shouted. 'I never done nothing. I'm a victim of brutality. I been wrong accused of this crime. I got mental conditions the police took advantage of.'

Hand-cuffed to two policemen Victor waited outside the line-up room. The detective came out.

'Good try, Victor.'

'You like that, Herbie?'

'Very good. You should of been in fucking films.'

'Sorry about the identification evidence, Herbie. As you say, I don't know what come over me. And here's you with all this evidence you can't use no more since my brief's going to get up on the hind legs in court and say your honour this here evidence is flawed because my client went and made a show of himself in front of the witnesses and that's why they're identifying him and after all the trouble you took.'

'Is that a fact Victor?'

'Afraid so. You see I always took this keen amateur interest in the law and it says all the people in a line-up's got to behave the same way. Still and all, it's good to see you take it generous.'

'The thing is Victor you're going to have to stay with us for a while till I get this sorted out and see if we can't come up with an accomplice and figure out a way to let him know that this running round the place, shooting everybody in sight, is not a very mature activity and maybe he'll tell us a story and maybe you being a famous person's going to be in this story.'

'That's very fucking comical, Herbie, you practise that or something?'

'Natural talent is all, Victor, natural talent.'

It was a shock to Dorcas when she heard that Victor was in the prison for murder. Although she knew that in times of rioting and disorder in the streets the police and courts were subject to errors in their thinking it never entered her mind that Victor would fall victim. It was exactly the ordeal a mother dreads. She was in a crippled apprehension for news in the first week but no information was forthcoming to her. Day after day she went to police stations to sit in grim thoughts while the police took not a blind bit of notice of her. The idea that she once placed faith in the police was a source of bitter laughter.

It was a normal thing in such circumstances to blame God

and be in dismay. But this was a temptation to which she resisted with all her might. Instead she took Big Ivan's suggestion that it was a case of mistaken identity. Though when Big Ivan said it first she felt at that moment that Victor was not himself but somebody else unknown. Or like identity withheld until next of kin are informed. She thought that it was a strange thing in families to become suddenly unknown to each other through thought or deed.

During those four weeks before he was released she had to go each Thursday on a minibus to visit, along with other women who had family in Crumlin Road. She did not wish to pass unnecessary judgement, but simply to say that some of them lacked anything which could be described as manners. She would pass over many of the things that came out of their mouths as words were not adequate. She was often fit for nothing by the time the minibus passed through the prison gate.

Being searched was a further tribulation, being sometimes required to remove garments, which was a large matter and not helped by the commonplace remarks of other women.

She regarded it as a sad matter for a mature woman to be in a place where men were caged like the beasts of the field. It recalled to her the cattle pens at the docks that were a part of her childhood, the pens being full of the sound of metal gates to wake the dead and a smell that rancoured in your nostrils as well. She thought at the time that all those animals bound for slaughter was an offence to innocence.

In addition it was not permitted by regulation to bring Victor a few small things of comfort, such as Tayto crisps or soda bread. There was also an atmosphere of damp to compare to their first house where clothes left in a wardrobe went mouldy overnight. It was an ease to her worry, though, that Victor was a Trustee prisoner from the start. Trust our Victor, she would say, and shake her head so that it could be seen that she was rueful but also proud.

When she went into the visiting room he was usually sat

there before her with that grin on that made you want to slap and also hug him. Of course she could not lay a hand across the table in light of warning notices that attempts to make physical contact will result in immediate termination of visit. At first it seemed that the desk where they sat was a great gulf separating mother and son. He was dark-skinned by nature but underneath he was pale. James told her once that sunlight was necessary to put vitamins in the skin. One of the foolish things he would say with the intention no doubt of putting the fear of God into her heart. A man who would go to football matches but would not come to visit his son. She knew there was nothing in it. But still a mother's natural woe.

Well son, she would always begin, and then they would sit there with nothing to say like persons who are facing a great jeopardy. She would feel as if her tongue and lips had betrayed her or that somehow words had been denied. She felt these encounters onerous. It was not something she could easily bear except that Victor seemed to have a light of understanding of this problem in his eye. At such times it seemed as if the whole room had stopped in a description of eternity. It occurred to her that speech itself is a cruel deceiver or kind of hoax which could not be relied upon. This fact was an ache felt in her breast. It left a taste as if of ashes in her mouth. When it seemed they had reached a pitch of silence to overtake endurance, a type of humming in the ears, Victor would find words like a man describing with hesitance a turning point in his life or a time he thought he would die but didn't. He told her the routine of his day, which did not vary. The quietness of his nights without a soul. She saw then that he would not go to seed or fall into brooding. Someone, he said, had told him how great men had found thoughts to guide them for the rest of their lives during dreary prison nights. The result was she felt assurance and when people on the street stopped to ask her, how's Victor? she was able to answer them with cheerfulness. Although she had misgivings from the start that the world would seek to thwart his high objective. It brought a nightly tear to her eye to think of him there in a dark cell turning things over in his head and perhaps going to the window to stare through the bars. She wondered if she had found the words to advise him would he have taken her advice so that she was not now heartrended.

seven

Ryan noticed how newspapers and television were developing a familiar and comforting vocabulary to deal with violence. Sentences which could be read easily off the page. It involved repetition of key phrases. Atrocity reports began to achieve the pure level of a chant. It was no longer about conveying information. It was about focusing the mind inwards, attending to the durable rhythms of violence.

Coppinger pointed out how the essential details of an attack, the things which differentiated one incident from another, were missing. Points which he considered vital were being omitted from eyewitness accounts. Whether the killer spoke the victim's name before firing. Whether or not the victim wore a mask, a combat jacket, a boilersuit. It was rare for paramilitaries to wear a stocking mask. It was a question of vanity. It made you look like an ancient bare-knuckle boxer. It suggested mild brain damage. Parkas were popular, berets, sunglasses. The black balaclava was a favourite and Coppinger held that this was due to commando films popular in the city. The Cockleshell Heroes.

They agreed that the reporting of violent incident was beginning to diverge from events. News editors had started to re-work their priorities, and government and intelligence agencies were at work. Paramilitaries escorted journalists to secret locations where they posed with general purpose machineguns and RPG7 rocket launchers. Car bombings were carried out to synchronize with news deadlines.

 had no grounds to hold him and he had felt that a big
as needed to mark his return. Big Ivan was behind the
etting up the large bottles of Red Hand as fast as he
 move. Victor was playing darts with Willie Lambe. The
as listening open-mouthed to Big Ivan's history of obscen-
 was late afternoon and they had been there since eleven
ck, sunshine coming in through the window. A day you
n't put the brakes on.

You and me, Victor,' Willie Lambe was saying, putting his
around Victor's shoulders. 'You and me, the best of mates,
?' He moved closer to Victor's ear. Victor laughed and
ed him away. Physical contact between men was a thing
isliked.

Willie had a scheme. He knew where they could rob a
er of alcohol from an industrial alcohol plant. They would
on it into 40-ounce Blue Smirnoff bottles and sell it to
pubs who'd take anything they could lay their greedy mitts
he knew that for a fact. The raw alcohol would cause
dness, impotence and other unknown symptoms exclusive
e destitute of heart.

'Armaggedon,' Willie whooped, 'the wrath of Victor.'

Victor recognized it as a bootleg plan which belonged on
uloid. Heavily laden trucks going without headlights on a
carious road skirting the edges of uncertainty. He had other
gs on his mind. The quiet face on Hacksaw McGrath after
 had done the two in the office. The fact that McGrath
n't been seen since. He had already got Big Ivan to ditch
weapons.

Heather watched them from the bar. When she liked she
ld withdraw into her mind so it was as if she wasn't there.
 thought of herself as disconnected at these moments.
 men treated her with absentminded gentleness. She was
only woman permitted to sit in at these gatherings. She
ld withdraw into the stance of a domestic mascot whose
sence bestowed indulgence without obligation.

When Victor was around Big Ivan treated Heather as an

Coppinger was following up incidents where the attackers
went unmasked.

'It means they're cocky bastards. It means they don't give
a shit if they get caught. Else it means they're protected
somehow.'

Ryan gave it a more ominous meaning. The killer was
compelled to form a liaison with the victim. To wear their fear
and disbelief like a garment of compulsive desire. It was the
full-screen close-up: the lips parted, the eyes half-closed, the
rapt expression.

It was eleven o'clock on Saturday morning when Coppinger
rang Ryan at his flat on the junction of the Antrim Road and
the Cavehill Road. Ryan had been drinking in the Markets the
night before. He had started to take on the role of the lone
drinker. He went to bars where he would not be recognized,
drinking heavily. He began to regard it as an austere calling,
demanding stamina and focus. After a while he started to
recognize others. Slight men around fifty years old with flecked
lips and watery red eyes as if from endless contemplation of
limited resources. Starting in the afternoon they moved from
bar to bar, having no more than one or two drinks in each.
Normally they sat beside a doorway, sometimes moving their
lips as if to address some verified and private rancour. He had
paid them little attention before although he had seen them
sitting in a packed bar at closing time or walking home with
their heads down. Contained, resentful, unhurried. It was the
most dangerous time of night. There was no activity on the
street and the men followed the same route each time. It
seemed like an invitation to violence, abduction, drive-past
shootings, but they were oblivious to the threat. They were
sunk in delusion and indifference and other devices of the
solitary.

Ryan began to walk home alone himself. Often taxis would
not come to the bars he frequented. Normally he would pass
through the city centre to the bottom of the Antrim Road. The
city centre had been heavily bombed with the emphasis on

commercial premises. These attacks had glamour. Damage estimates running into six figures were quoted with admiration, part of an awesome and impersonal civic expenditure.

Once he had gone from Royal Avenue to the Antrim Road the dereliction was on a more intimate scale. Acres of pre-war housing had been abandoned because of intimidation. The windows and doorways had been bricked up. The official explanation for this was to prevent vandalism and arson, but Ryan always felt an overwhelming sense of violently interrupted lives when he walked past. He imagined the houses kept spotlessly clean, the doorsteps worn from scrubbing. It was a dark place. These streets retained a sense of worked lives. It was for this that the windows and doors were bricked, to restrain vengeful domestic spirits.

Often he passed small groups of youths, a metallic taste of alcohol in his mouth. His walk was a drunk's precarious experiment with motion, a struggle with memory. He felt it offered immunity. It drew on an ancient respect for the afflicted and infirm. The youths wore Wrangler jackets and parallel jeans. He could not anticipate their reactions. You had to know the structure of the gang. The implacable codes.

When the telephone rang he was looking at himself in the bathroom mirror. Attempting to distinguish age and damage from the glass's liverspots and seeping watermarks. He wondered how long it would take before he began to resemble the men who drifted from pub to pub. The bleakness. The dark thought that no longer beholds itself.

'O'Neill's Car Parts warehouse,' Coppinger said. He pronounced each word carefully and Ryan knew that he had been drinking. He thought of a pilot losing altitude, a last positional report.

'The location is right for our boys. Between the Falls and the Shankill. Easy access. Four men without masks. There are four dead, two men shot in the back of the head while in a kneeling position.'

'Robbery?'

'There's no money missing as far as police Apparently all they took was two headlights f job Capri.' bar

'What makes you think it's the same peo could jobs?' bar

'I'm telling you, you go sniffing about this ity. I who done this one there'll be a massive b o'clo nobody talking. People looking over their sh could making excuses not to meet you. There's some

'What?' arm

'The two men made to kneel.' right

'What? Prayer? Attitude of submission.' push

'Something there yes, and no money too he d Except the headlights. Too impatient to rob the bodies all over the place and somebody thinking tank headlight for the car, I'll have that. There's blo syph There's a smell of cordite and this fucker's takin Taig

'Petty.' on,

'Yes.' blin

'Doesn't give a shit.' to t

'No. Something else.'

'Gratuitous.'

'That's not it. It's the calculation in it. The cell dead.' pre

'Maybe.' thir

There was a wistful pause in which they were the of the telephone line between them, miles of res ha The speech of the city. A dreamtime of voices. A r the on the line like the vexed, insistent voices of the was still holding the receiver in his hand minutes a co ger had hung up, dried shaving foam on his face. Sh off with a towel and ran the hot tap again. Please. I The the wo pre

Victor and his team were in the Pot Luck celebrating job. Following the collapse of the identification ev accomplice in matters of love and consulted her on the doings of women. It was a perpetual problem for him. He put his longing on furtive display for her like some valuable treasure removed by looters, a fragile reliquary with associations of national yearning. Big Ivan acted as if it had fallen unwanted into his hands. He wanted to make amends for possessing it.

Willie Lambe kept a photograph of his mother on the dashboard of his car. His mother was twenty years old in the photograph, pretty, with a skin that suggested lacquer. Willie showed Victor the photograph. She looks like a film star from a silent picture, Victor said. Louise Brooks. Some malnourished heroine fading out of earshot. Victor laughed when Heather asked him about the mother. Fucking acts like she's a film star too, he said. He had been in the house which Willie shared with his mother. She was surrounded by photographs of herself in her youth. The photographs were arranged in groups on small tables. There were themes of gaiety, companionship, eternal youth. She smoked white-tipped menthol cigarettes, and the butts coated in lipstick smouldered in gift ashtrays. She was a fucking dried-up old hag who treated Willie like a slave, Victor said. Willie wags the tail when she pats the head, he said. Themes of cruelty, maternal neglect.

Heather noticed that each time Victor established a pattern he would break it. He would stay two or three nights at her flat then disappear for days. He never travelled by the same route. He never fucked her the same way twice in a row. He arrived with unexpected gifts. He would awake from varied nightmares. A gift for survival, he called it, secrets of a fugitive heart. One night he told her how John Dillinger had undergone plastic surgery to avoid detection. Victor was deeply impressed by the possibilities of transformation. To see yourself altered beyond recognition in a mirror. Heather said imagine looking in the mirror and seeing a squint and a double chin. Imagine seeing Big Ivan. I like you the way you are, she said.

Victor told her to continue with the parties in the flat. He explained to her that McClure was compiling dossiers. He showed her photographs that McClure had given him. She realized that many of them had been taken in her own flat. There were naked bodies on floors and in beds. They seemed unsurprised by the flashlight, as if the sight of each other's bodies had already confirmed sorrowful predictions. There were tapes as well, which he played on the car stereo. These were full of noises of sad recognition, a bleak interior language in which it seemed that irretrievable losses were being mourned.

McClure had policemen, civil servants and intelligence personnel in his portfolio. It was a case of finding a vice and exploiting it. He explained to Victor that he was concerned with extending the limits of human tolerance, pushing the victims of blackmail to the edge of logic. There had been suicides, which he regarded as defeat.

McClure had introduced Victor to amphetamine. Using a knife he had cut the top off a Benzidrex nasal inhaler and removed the cotton insert which he tore in half. He gave one piece to Victor, showing him how to dip it in milk to deaden its bitter chemical taste with overtones of dumped chemicals, slow leakage and genetic damage.

They spent the afternoon in a house on Crimea Street. Victor remembered sun in the room elaborated through the nylon net curtains on the small window, a sustaining lightfall. It seemed that they employed the speech of a seemly diplomacy — fluent protocols exchanged across a table by soft-spoken men whose words were accompanied by elegant gestures of goodwill. McClure made strong black coffee to boost the amphetamine. Their words had a soft gleam of meaning. Victor explained the discrimination he had suffered from, being mistaken for a Catholic because of the name Kelly. Their detestation of Catholics was a companionable thing. They agreed upon it as a resource requiring careful nurture.

McClure explained his attraction to the Nazis. Their elimination of remorse. The doctrinal simplicity. The massed voices and hushed stadiums. The defined oratorical sorrows.

He opened a cupboard and showed Victor a book which had been produced in Berlin in 1940. The German title was printed in heavy Gothic type, sharp-edged alien characters which seemed beyond anything that could be shaped by the palate. Each page had a single photographic plate of a nude boy who stared at the camera with a sombre, violated gaze.

'People's looking for control,' McClure said. 'They want somebody to take over, decide things for them, what to do with their lives. They'll hand over their life and cry tears of fucking gratitude that somebody else'll take it on for them. All that misery and deciding. They want to dress up and act the hero and fuck the rest. They'll die for that.'

Victor heard music approaching down the road. They went to the front door. Orangemen were returning from the dedication of a new banner, accompanied by several flute bands. The Orangemen walked in ranks between the bands wearing orange silk collarettes and black bowler hats. Two of them carried the banner showing William of Orange on a white charger. Their faces seemed distorted to Victor, as if they had witnessed some corrosive spectacle. The sunlight struck the metal fittings of the drums and flutes and the flute-players dipped their instruments to the rhythm of the march.

eight

I John McGrath would like to state that the events I describe in the following happened as if in a dream so that it was as if I did not participate although I know that I did and this is a source of regret to me. We drove up to the gate of O'Neill's depot at ten o'clock in the morning of 10 May 1975. I remember a sign Trade Only at the gate which gave me a moment of panic at being recognized as not being trade. I felt foreign to my own nature from that moment. We stopped the car at the entrance to the warehouse. We got out and walked in. Mr C's eyes were lit up and he looked from side to side as if his head was afflicted by madness which I also started to feel, although I had no notion of a bloodbath at this or any other point. I do not wish to give the full name of Mr C.

There was another man with us who I also do not wish to name as he is notorious for being involved in killing and has not a spark of mercy in his nature. This man I shall call Mr M. He had wrote out this car parts order which was a fake on a piece of paper tore from a children's exercise book. He seemed to be in high good spirits at this point. Two assistants came up to us and Mr M handed one the note but before they could read it Mr C had them covered with a gun he took from his pocket and he said lie down on the ground. They lay down at that point.

Then Mr M said where's the office? One of the assistants looked up at us and pointed. I would like to say that there was no look of fear on his face or on the other one's. They seemed to lie down in a kind of blind disbelief. I remember Mr C said we should've brought a van and took some of the car parts that were sitting round the place but M said we were there for the money. M kept looking at me and saying things like are you all right and smiling at me to make me feel part of things. Apart from the incident with Frames which was a mistake with a gun going off by accident this was the first time I ever done anything like that and I hope I will never be involved again. This is a statement of my remorse.

M indicated that I should go with him to the office. I cannot remember how he said it or if he used words at all. We went up these old wooden steps which creaked with a noise to wake the dead. M seemed to change somehow as we went up as if it was a climb to murder. He had these blue eyes which seemed to get smaller and he did not speak.

The office had two glass windows looking over the depot and a glass door. There were two men inside. They looked up and seen me and M outside the glass. You could see them looking nervous and talking to each other but you couldn't hear them through the glass. Seeing them and all it was still like they weren't really there. It was like watching an event that happened some time ago recorded. M opened the door and we went in.

I had never been in a proper office before and it was just like you imagined a real one, or one on television. There were green filing cabinets and a desk with this big typewriter on it. I had this notion to type my name on it like a typist with big fingernails but M saw me and said not to do it.

The older man came forward and asked what we wanted. He had grey hair and was like your uncle or someone you know well who gives you that look like he was disappointed in you but not surprised to tell the truth. M said that we come for the money and that we were serious. He said it was early on Monday morning and that there was no money yet in a voice like everybody knows that. The younger one didn't say nothing but just looked at us. I am sorry for the younger one. M said for them both to kneel on the floor. The older man looked at him and he said it again to kneel.

I am of the belief now that robbery was not the motive for the actions of M on that day and that he had the whole thing planned from the start. There have been questions as to the mental state of M in that period and I would like to state that there was no sign of madness from when we reached the office but that he was calm and smiling during the incidents described.

When they were kneeling on the floor with their backs to us M put his gun to the older man's neck and I put my gun to the younger man's neck who started to say something. I think it was a Roman Catholic prayer. This seemed to cause displeasure to M. He fired his gun and mine went off also. I remember nothing of the office after that except that there was more smoke from the guns than you would think and that it gave you a taste in your mouth like when you touch a battery with your tongue to see if there is still any power left in it.

We went out of the office. Downstairs we saw that the other two were shot as well. M went behind the counter and looked until he saw headlights for his car. There was much laughter and talk in the car on the way back and no mention of the money. M said that I done well but I knew what would happen if I opened my mouth. I wish to say that I have now embraced Christian values and express repugnance at my deeds and that having made this clean breast I am at ease now in Christ.